FOOTBALL
AND OTHER BALL GAMES
by Jason Page

LOOK OUT!

The fastest baseball pitchers can throw the ball at a speed of more than 150 km/h.

ANCIENT ORIGINS

From football to table tennis, and softball to hockey, the Olympic ball games are some of the most varied and exciting sports at the Games!

OLYMPIC HISTORY

Many of the ball games played at the modern Olympic Games have ancient origins. Hockey is one of the oldest sports in the world and this stone carving shows a hockey game in ancient Greece. Roman soldiers sometimes played football — only they used the heads of their enemies rather than a ball!

A hockey game in ancient Greece

SUPER STATS

Here are the diameters of some of the balls used at the Games. You can see that they come in many different sizes!

Table tennis ball
— 3.8 cm;
Hockey ball
— 7 cm;
Softball
— 10 cm;
Football
— 22 cm;
Basketball
— 24 cm.

STRIKING GOLD

Modern Olympians are dedicated athletes who spend countless hours training in preparation for the Games. But at the first Olympics, things were rather different. In 1896, the first-ever tennis gold medal was won by John Pius Boland (GBR), who went along to watch the Games as a spectator and decided to have a go himself at the last minute!

WATCH THIS SPACE

The ball games at the 2008 Olympics will take place in many different venues. One of these is the Wukesong Baseball Field, which has three diamonds just for the one event! For football, the early rounds will take place in other cities.

OLYMPICS FACT FILE

🎵 The Olympic Games were first held in Olympia, in ancient Greece, around 3,000 years ago. They took place every four years until they were abolished in 393 CE.

🎵 A Frenchman called Pierre de Coubertin (1863–1937) revived the Games, and the first modern Olympics were held in Athens in 1896.

🎵 The modern Games have been held every four years since 1896, except in 1916, 1940 and 1944, because of war. Special 10th-anniversary Games took place in 1906.

🎵 The symbol of the Olympic Games is five interlocking coloured rings. Together, they represent the five different continents from which athletes come to compete.

NEW SPORTS

Not all of the Olympic ball games have such an impressive family history. Some, such as softball, are relatively new. Like several other games, softball was invented in the last century. However, it will only be making its fourth ever appearance at the Games in Beijing.

**Softball player
(US women's team)**

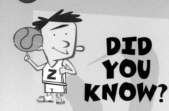

DID YOU KNOW?

‽ The greatest victory (or worst defeat, depending on which team you support!) in a handball match occurred in 1980, when Yugoslavia beat Kuwait 44–10.

‽ The first handball players were football players who took up the sport as a way of keeping fit during the 'off season'.

‽ The ball used in women's matches is slightly smaller and lighter than the one used in men's games.

HANDBALL HISTORY

The ancient Romans and Greeks played a game which was very similar to handball. However, the rules of the modern game were not drawn up until 1917. Handball first appeared at the Olympic Games in 1936, when it was played outside with teams of 11 players. It reappeared as an indoor 7-a-side sport in 1972 and has been part of the Olympic Games ever since.

Goalkeeper restraining line – the goalkeeper is no allowed to cross this line when trying to save a penalty.

Goal area line – only the goalkeeper is allowed inside the goal area but attacking players may jump over the line and shoot at goal while in mid-air.

Handball pitch

Seong-Ok Oh (KOR)

WHAT A MATCH!

Seong-Ok Oh (KOR) takes a flying shot at Denmark's goal during the women's final at the 1996 Olympics. The match was one of the closest and most exciting in the history of the Games. Denmark was awarded a penalty just before the final buzzer, but a heroic save by the Korean goalkeeper meant that the full-time score was a draw. The match then went to extra time where the Danes pulled off a surprise victory over the Koreans.

HANDBALL

Handball is based on the rules of soccer. The big difference is that you use your hands, not your feet, to control the ball!

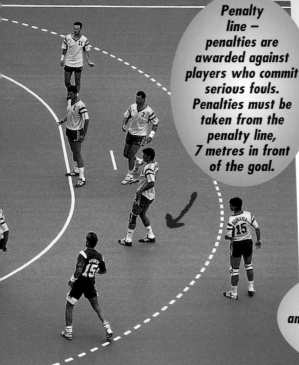

Penalty line – penalties are awarded against players who commit serious fouls. Penalties must be taken from the penalty line, 7 metres in front of the goal.

RULE BOOK

The aim is to score as many points as possible by throwing the ball into the opposition's goal. Players are only allowed to hold on to the ball for 3 seconds, or take 3 paces with it, before they must pass, shoot or bounce it on the ground. Only the goalkeeper is allowed to touch the ball with his feet.

Free throw line – if a defending player commits a foul between this line and the goal area, the attacking side are given a free throw from the edge of the dotted line.

SPEEDOMETER

Handball is a fast and physical game. Players throw the ball through the air at speeds of up to 100 km/h – the speed the fastest birds can fly!

TENNIS

Although tennis was included in the first-ever modern Olympics in 1896, it was left out of the Games in 1928 and was not included again as a full medal sport until 1988.

WIMBLEDON WINNERS

A total of 29 Olympic gold medal winners have also won the Lawn Tennis Championships at Wimbledon — the most prestigious 'grand slam' tennis tournament. They include Andre Agassi, who won the men's singles at Wimbledon in 1992 and an Olympic gold in 1996.

GOING TO GROUND

The tennis courts used at the Games in Beijing will have a high-tech rubberized hard court surface that's designed to suit all playing styles.

LEARN THE LINGO

Ace – a winning serve which the other player fails to hit

Love – zero points

Deuce – when both players have 40 points

Fault – a serve falling outside the service lines; players serving two faults in a row lose the point

Let – this means the point must be played again

A modern graphite tennis racket

Andre Agassi (USA)

WHAT A RACKET

Tennis rackets must be no longer than 73.66 cm and no wider than 31.75 cm, but there are no rules about what shape they should be or what they should be made from! The first rackets were made of wood and their 'heads' (the part with strings) were wider on one side than the other. Modern rackets have an oval head and are made of new materials such as graphite that are both light and strong.

GOLDEN GIRLS

In 1900, tennis became the first Olympic sport in which women were able to compete. The first-ever female gold medallist was Charlotte Cooper (GBR), who won the women's singles.

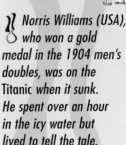

DID YOU KNOW?

❥ Norris Williams (USA), who won a gold medal in the 1904 men's doubles, was on the Titanic when it sunk. He spent over an hour in the icy water but lived to tell the tale.

❥ Modern tennis was invented by Major Walter Clopton Wingfield in 1874 – although he called it 'sphairistike'!

❥ Andre Agassi's father competed in the Olympics as a boxer representing Iran.

Venus and Serena Williams (USA)

WILLIAMS WINNING

With 22 Grand Slam titles between them, there are not many tennis events left for Venus and Serena Williams to conquer. The two have often competed against each other, but in 2000, the sisters joined forces to win gold in the women's doubles at the Sydney Olympics. If that wasn't enough, Venus Williams went onto to win the women's single gold medal at the same Games!

The net must be exactly 91.4 cm high in the centre of the court.

When a player is serving, the ball must land in the opponent's service area opposite.

Women's doubles

DID YOU KNOW?

Tennis balls at the Olympics are stored in a refrigerator until they are ready to be used. This ensures that they are all equally bouncy!

Players automatically lose a point if they touch the ball with their body or if they touch the net.

Until 1924, there was a 'mixed doubles' event at the Olympics with a male and female player in each team.

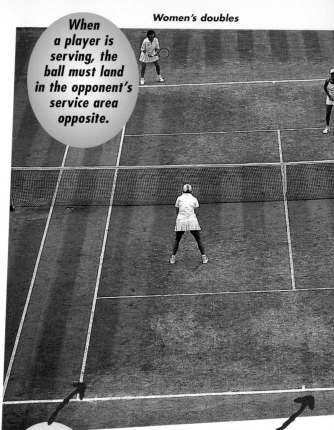

The inner sidelines mark the edge in singles matches.

The base line marks the furthest edge of the court. A ball landing beyond this line (or the sidelines) on its first bounce is 'out'.

TENNIS (CONTINUED)

As well as the singles tennis events, there are also doubles events in which two players play as a team.

ON THE BALL

There are strict rules about the size of tennis balls used in the Olympics. They must measure 6.54–6.85 cm in diameter and weigh 56.7–58.5 g. When dropped from a height of 254 cm onto a concrete floor, they must bounce between 134.62 cm and 147.32 cm.

NATIONAL BOUNDARIES

In the early modern Games, doubles teams were often made up of two players from different countries. Now, all doubles partners must have the same nationality and only one team is allowed per country.

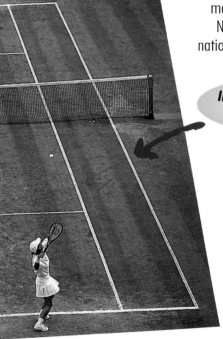

In doubles matches the outer sidelines are used to make the court wider.

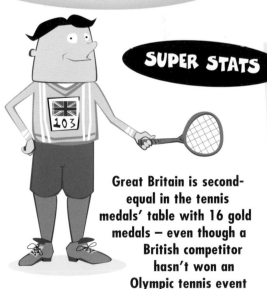

SUPER STATS

Great Britain is second-equal in the tennis medals' table with 16 gold medals – even though a British competitor hasn't won an Olympic tennis event since 1920! The USA also has 16 golds.

The men's doubles were won in 2004 by Sébastien Lareau and Daniel Nestor (CAN). They beat the 1996 winners, Todd Woodbridge and Mark Woodforde (AUS).

BASKETBALL

Modern basketball was invented by an American, Dr James Naismith, in 1891 – and the USA has dominated the sport ever since.

RACE AGAINST TIME

Michael Jordan (USA)

Basketball players must play against the clock as well as their opponents. As soon as one team takes possession of the ball, they have just 10 seconds to move into their opponents' half of the court and 30 seconds to try to score, otherwise the ball automatically goes to the other side.

SUPER STATS

The men's basketball event has been held 16 times at the Games and the USA has won it 12 times so far. The women's event has been held only eight times and the USA has already notched up five victories.

USA	17
USSR/Russia	5
Yugoslavia	1
Argentina	1

Players may only run with the ball if they bounce it with one hand at every step. This is called dribbling. If a player stops moving, he cannot start dribbling again but must pass or shoot. Here, Michael Jordan (USA) shows how it's done during the 1992 Olympic final.

REIGNING OLYMPIC CHAMPIONS: Men's event: ARGENTINA

WHAT'S THE SCORE?

When you watch a basketball game, you'll notice there's a wide, curved line around the basket at each end of the court. This is called the three-point arc.

If players throw the ball into the basket from beyond this line, they score three points; scoring from within the line is worth only two points. The most spectacular way to score is to take a massive leap and thrust the ball into the basket from above — this is known as a 'slam dunk'.

DEADLY GAME

A game similar to modern-day basketball was first played more than 500 years ago in Mexico by the Aztecs. The aim was to get a ball made of rubber through a raised stone hoop (right). The Aztecs took their sport very seriously — at the end of a match, all the members of the losing team were put to death!

Aztec basketball hoop

VOLLEYBALL

There are two volleyball events at the Olympics — indoor volleyball and beach volleyball. First, we'll take a look at indoor volleyball.

ALL CHANGE

An indoor volleyball team is made up of six players — three at the front of the court and three at the back. Every time a team wins the right to serve, all the players on that team must change position, rotating clockwise around the court. The ball must be served by the player nearest the right-hand corner at the back of the court. This player must stand behind the baseline to hit the ball over the net.

LEARN THE LINGO

Bump –
a pass made using
the forearm

Side out –
when a team loses
the right to serve

Attack zone –
the front half
of the court

Spike –
a smash shot from
above the net

NICE TOUCH

Players are allowed to use any part of their bodies to control the ball, including their feet. However, once a player has touched the ball, that player may not touch it again until it has been hit by another player. Each team is allowed no more than three hits of the ball in a row and players are forbidden to touch the net.

Two new rules were introduced for the first time at the 2000 Sydney Games. One is that players will now score a point every time they land the ball on their opponents' side of the court — regardless of who served the ball. The other allows a special substitute player, called a 'libero', to replace one of the players on the back row — it is hoped this will encourage longer rallies!

Women's final 2004: China versus Russia

DID YOU KNOW?

Volleyball was invented in 1895 by William Morgan. He was a friend of Dr James Naismith, the man who invented basketball.

Originally, Morgan called volleyball 'mintonette', but it's not known why he chose this name.

A line divides each half of the court across the middle. The three players at the back of the court are only allowed to spike the ball if they jump from behind this line.

ON THE ATTACK

1. The first stage in a classic volleyball attack is for one player to pass the ball to a team-mate near the net.

2. This player then 'sets the ball' by punching it up into the air.

3. A third player then completes the move, leaping above the net and smashing the ball down into the opponents' court — this move is known as a 'spike'.

DID YOU KNOW?

Beach volleyball was invented in California in the 1920s.

The volleyball net is slightly higher in the men's competitions – 2.43 metres compared with 2.24 metres in the women's volleyball events.

In beach volleyball, blocking an opponent's shot counts as one of your team's three hits of the ball; this rule doesn't apply to indoor volleyball.

SAME DIFFERENCE?

As with indoor volleyball, each team may hit the ball no more than three times in a row. Each time players handle the ball, they must either pass it to their team-mate or hit it over the net. However, the scoring system for beach volleyball is slightly different. Only the team who served the ball at the start of the rally can win a point. If they lose the rally, they lose the serve to the other team.

Emanuel Rego and Ricardo Alex Santos (BRA) celebrate winning the men's beach volleyball at the 2004 Olympic Games.

REIGNING OLYMPIC CHAMPIONS: Men's beach volleyball: BRAZIL

VOLLEY ALL
(CONTINUED)

Beach volleyball made its first appearance at the Games in 1996, and has since been one of the most popular Olympic events.

TWO'S COMPANY

In beach volleyball, there are just two players in each team. This picture shows one half of the reigning women's Olympic champions, Kerri Walsh, who with Misty May (USA), won gold medals at the 2004 Athens Games. Since beach volleyball became an Olympic event, Brazil has won 5 medals and the USA and Australia have won two each.

LEARN THE LINGO

Roof – a block used to stop an attempted 'spike'

Dig – saving a low ball and hitting it back up into the air

Kill – any attacking shot that is unreturnable

Assist – passing the ball to a player for a 'kill'

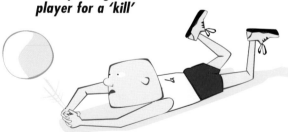

LIFE'S A BEACH

The dimensions of a beach volleyball court are identical to an indoor volleyball court, including the height of the net. The only difference is the surface – this game is played outside on a beach! Because the wind and weather can make a big difference to a game, players are required to change halves every five points.

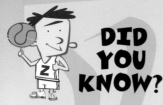

DID YOU KNOW?

♬ *Members of the batting side are allowed to 'steal' bases by suddenly sprinting to the next base when the fielding team aren't looking.*

♬ *The longest-ever throw by a fielder in a baseball game measured 135.88 metres!*

♬ *If the ball thrown by the pitcher hits the batter, the batter is allowed to walk to the next base, unopposed.*

YOU'RE OUT!

There are three ways to get a batter out:

1. He can be caught out if he hits the ball and a fielder catches it before it lands.

2. He can be struck out if he fails to hit the ball properly after three attempts.

3. He can be put out if a fielder touches him with the ball while he is running from one base to another, or if a fielder with the ball gets to the base before him.

1,2,3,4
First base, second base, third base and home base respectively.

6
Everything inside this square is known as the infield.

5
Pitcher's mound – a mound of earth 40 cm high where the 'pitcher' (the player who throws the ball to the batter) stands.

7
Foul lines – the batter cannot score if he hits the ball outside these two lines.

Outfield

ASEBALL

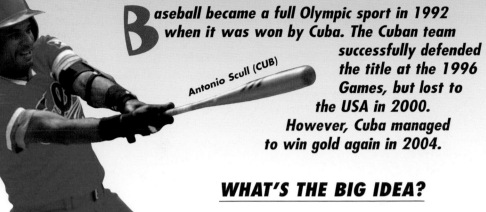

Baseball became a full Olympic sport in 1992 when it was won by Cuba. The Cuban team successfully defended the title at the 1996 Games, but lost to the USA in 2000. However, Cuba managed to win gold again in 2004.

Antonio Scull (CUB)

WHAT'S THE BIG IDEA?

Only men can compete in the Olympic baseball events. Players score points by hitting the ball, then running from one 'base' to the next until they return to the home base where they started. Teams are made up of nine players who take it in turns to bat and to field, swapping around every time the fielding side get three of their opponents out. Once both teams have had nine goes at batting, the one with the most runs is the winner.

ESSENTIAL EQUIPMENT

Baseball bats are made of wood or aluminium and have smooth, rounded sides. The ball is about the same size as a tennis ball but much harder; it's made of cork or rubber with a leather skin. Batsmen wear plastic helmets to protect their heads while players on the fielding side are allowed to use large leather gloves, called 'mitts', to help them catch the ball.

SPEEDOMETER

The fastest baseball pitchers can throw the ball at more than 150 km/h – that's faster than a family car going at top speed!

SOFTBALL

*T*he 2008 Olympics will be the last time women's softball appears at the Olympic Games unless it is reinstated at a later date. The International Olympic Committee decided to have the sport removed.

A hard plastic helmet protects the player's head.

Catching mitt

Body pad

Softball catcher

SPOT THE DIFFERENCE

Softball was invented as an indoor version of baseball but there are some important differences:

1. Only women play softball at Olympic level (baseball is played by men).

2. The ball used in softball is larger, but the pitch is smaller than that used in baseball.

3. In softball games, the pitcher must throw the ball underarm (overarm in baseball).

4. Softball players are not allowed to 'steal' a base until the pitcher throws the ball, but they can do this at any time in baseball.

5. In softball, each side gets seven turns at batting compared with nine in baseball.

SPEEDOMETER

The fastest softball pitch recorded at an Olympics was in Atlanta, when the ball shot through the air at more than 118 km/h – that's faster than a sailfish, the speediest creature on Earth.

NOT SO SOFT

There's nothing soft about softball! In fact, the person batting actually needs faster reactions than a baseball batter, because although the ball isn't pitched quite as fast in softball, the pitcher stands much closer — which means the batter has less time to react!

Face guard

Softball players

One player, called the catcher, crouches on the fielding team behind the batter. The catcher's job is to catch the ball thrown by the pitcher if the batter misses it, and to defend the home base. The catcher needs to wear plenty of protective gear, as this picture shows.

AMERICA ALL-STARS

The USA softball team once played 106 games over nine years without losing a match. Their phenomenal winning streak came to a temporary end when they were defeated by China in 1995. However, a year later the USA won the first-ever softball medal, and has won every gold medal in the event since!

Knee and shin pads

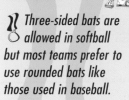

DID YOU KNOW?

Three-sided bats are allowed in softball but most teams prefer to use rounded bats like those used in baseball.

Softball is the most popular participation sport in the USA and is played by more than 20 million people worldwide.

Softball was originally called 'kitten-ball' and 'mush-ball'!

DID YOU KNOW?

Table tennis has been known by many names, including gossima, whiff-whaff, flim-flam and ping-pong.

More people play table tennis than any other sport in the world: there are over 40 million competitive players — plus those who just play for fun!

In table tennis, players are not allowed to hit the ball until it has bounced on the table in front of them.

COMPLETELY BATTY

Table tennis bats can be any size or shape as long as 85 percent of the bat is made of wood. Each side of a bat is covered with a pimpled rubber surface (no thicker than 2 mm), or a layer of spongy foam faced with pimpled rubber (no thicker than 4 mm). These outer coatings enable the players to hit the ball much faster.

The reigning men's Olympic champion, Ryu Seung-Min (KOR).

Yaping Deng (CHN)

GET A GRIP

The 1996 Olympic champion, Yaping Deng (CHN), holds the bat in an unusual grip called the 'shake hands' grip. Most players (especially other Chinese players) use a grip called the 'pen hold' grip.

TABLE TENNIS

Table tennis made its first appearance at the Games in 1988. Since then, it has proved that you don't need a big bat to be a big hit!

HISTORY LESSON

Table tennis was invented during the late 1800s and soon became a popular after-dinner game. The first players used a ball carved from a champagne cork and cigar box lids for bats. By the early 1900s, toy companies had started making proper bats and balls.

SUPER STATS

China has won more gold medals than any other nation in the table tennis events, with a grand total of 16. In second place is South Korea with three, while Sweden is third with one.

China	16
South Korea	3
Sweden	1

WHAT'S THE POINT?

Players win a point every time they hit a valid shot that their opponent can't return. The winner is the first player to reach 21 points but players must beat their opponent by at least two points. So, if one player has 21 points and the other has 20, the first player still needs an extra point to win.

Women's singles: Zhang Yining (CHN)

TABLE TENNIS
(CONTINUED)

*J*ust like lawn tennis, table tennis also has a doubles tournament in which two players play together.

Each table tennis match at the Olympics is watched over by an umpire who sits on a raised chair in line with the net. This give them a bird's-eye view of the game. Other judges watch for faults.

Table tennis doubles match

SPEEDOMETER

LT88

Despite its small size, a table tennis ball whizzes across the table at speeds of up to 170 km/h — that's faster than a small plane can travel!

AT YOUR SERVICE

When serving in table tennis, players must throw the ball at least 16 cm into the air and hit it as it falls back down. Their shot must also bounce on both sides of the net. In singles matches, players are allowed to serve to and from any part of the table, but in doubles games the ball must be hit diagonally across the table from one right hand corner to the other.

SKILLS & SHOTS

Table tennis requires lightning reactions and great co-ordination. Players need to master a number of different shots, including slices (which make the ball spin off at unexpected angles) and smashes (which wallop the ball down onto the opponents' side of the table with great force).

DID YOU KNOW?

♫ Table tennis balls must be orange or white. They weigh just 2.5 g — that's 18 times lighter than a golf ball!

♫ China won all of the gold medals awarded in the table tennis events at the last Olympic Games except for one!

♫ Certain glues used to make table tennis bats are banned at the Olympics because they can make the ball travel up to 30 km/h faster than ordinary glues!

TAKING TURNS

In doubles games, the players must hit the ball in strict rotation. The server hits it to the receiver who hits it to the server's partner, who then hits it to the receiver's partner who hits it back to the server. If a player hits the ball out of turn, their team loses the point.

Chen Qi and Ma Lin (CHN)

JOLLY HOCKEY STICKS

Tycho van Meer (NED) & Jaime Amat (ESP)

Hockey is a bit like football. The aim is to score goals by hitting the ball into the other team's goal. Hockey sticks are shaped like long hooks. Their curved ends are flat on one side and rounded on the other. Players may only hit the ball with the flat side of their stick and, except for the goalie, may not touch the ball with any part of their body.

Helmet with face guard

Elbow pads

DID YOU KNOW?

♫ The term 'hockey' is thought to come from the French word 'hoquet' (which means a shepherd's crook), because of its curved shape.

♫ Hockey is played on a pitch 91.4 metres long and 55 metres wide, which is slightly smaller than a football pitch. Each team is made up of 11 players.

♫ Four different Indian players all called Balbir Singh have won medals in the men's hockey events at the Olympics.

Hockey stick – the goalkeeper is allowed to throw or kick the ball, as well as hit it with his hockey stick.

ANCIENT ORIGINS

Hockey is one of the oldest known sports. In fact, it was played in Egypt more than 1,000 years before the first Olympic Games were held in ancient Greece. The modern rules of field hockey (its proper name) were drawn up in 1886. The men's hockey event was held for the first time at the modern Olympics in 1908.

Large pads protect the goalkeeper's legs.

HOCKEY

Hockey may be more ancient than the Olympic Games but it's been brought bang up-to-date with an exciting new rule!

> The goalkeeper is allowed to use any part of their body to block a shot.

WHAT'S NEW?

A new rule introduced for the first time at the Games in Sydney said that attacking players can no longer be offside — meaning that players can now score from any position on the pitch. The purpose of this new rule is to encourage more goals.

SUPER STATS

India holds eight gold medals in the hockey events — that's more than any other country. It won every single final from 1928 to 1956. In second place is Australia with four golds and in joint-third are Great Britain, Pakistan and the Netherlands.

FOOTBALL

Football will be the only Olympic sport to be played before the Games officially begin in Beijing. The first two matches will be played before the opening ceremony!

The Nigerian team are all smiles after defeating Argentina in the football final at the 1996 Games. It was the first time that a team from Africa had won the event.

The Nigerian football team

LEARN THE LINGO

Red card – if a player commits a serious offence, they are shown a red card and sent off the pitch by the referee

Striker – an attacking player

Winger – a player who plays down the sides of the pitch

Sweeper – a defensive player whose job is to clear the ball away from the goal

BANNED!

Football is the only Olympic sport ever to have been banned by royal decree. In the thirteenth century, King Edward II outlawed football in England because he was afraid that his subjects were spending too much time kicking a ball about when they should have been practising their archery skills. However, no one took much notice of the king and 800 years later, football has become the world's favourite sport!

REIGNING OLYMPIC CHAMPIONS: Men's: ARGENTINA

KICKING OFF

At the 2008 Games, 16 men's teams and 12 women's teams will take part in the football events. Professional players can take part in the men's competition but teams are only allowed three players who are over 23 years old. The women's competition, first held in 1996, is open to players aged over 16.

DID YOU KNOW?

The US women's team are the reigning world champions in the women's competition, and are favourites to win the gold medal in Beijing.

Danish centre forward Sophus Nielsen scored 10 goals in 1908, when Denmark defeated France 17–1.

Football and water polo were the first-ever team sports to be introduced to the modern Olympics. They became part of the Games in 1900.

KICKING ABOUT

Not all of the football events will be played in the city of Beijing at the 2008 Olympic Games. Many of them will be played in Shenyang, the capital city of the Liaoning province in northeast China. The brand new Shenyang Olympic Sports Centre, pictured left, is being built for the Games.

Women's: USA

DID YOU KNOW?

♫ *Badminton players can run up to 6 km during a match.*

♫ *A 'kill' in badminton is a shot hit into the opponent's court that cannot be returned.*

♫ *Badminton made its Olympic debut in 1992.*

GAME & MATCH

In badminton, the first person or team to win two games wins the match. To win a game in the women's singles, players need at least 11 points, while 15 points are the minimum required in all the other events.

HOW TO SERVE

Players serve by dropping the shuttle and hitting it as it falls. They may only serve underarm while standing still with both feet on the ground, and the shuttle must be struck below the waist. In badminton, only the player who serves can win a point.

THE ONE THAT GOT AWAY

Asian countries lead the world when it comes to badminton. China, Korea and Indonesia have won all of the gold medals in the badminton events in the last four Olympics — except for one. The exception was the 1996 men's singles gold medalist, Paul-Erik Hoyer-Larsen (DEN).

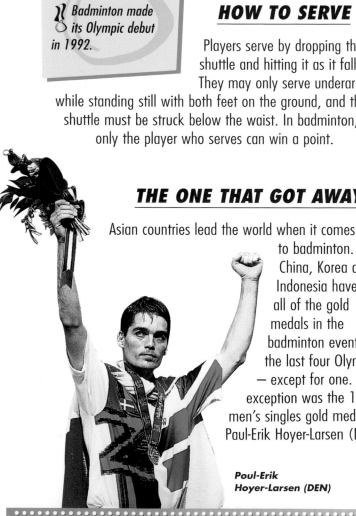

Poul-Erik Hoyer-Larsen (DEN)

BADMINTON

Badminton is like a ball game — but without the ball! It first appeared at the Olympic Games in 1992.

FEATHER POWER

Badminton isn't really a ball game at all. It's played with a super-speedy missile made from cork and goose feathers, called a 'shuttlecock' — or 'shuttle' for short. The aim is to score points by hitting the shuttle over the net so that it lands in the opponent's service court.

LEARN THE LINGO

Drive – an attacking shot played from the centre of the court

Lob – a high shot that goes over the opponent's head and lands at the back of the court

Drop shot – a low power shot that just clears the net then falls to the ground

Round the head – a forehand shot played over the top of the head

Retrieving a drop shot – Camilla Martin (DEN)

BADMINTON
(CONTINUED)

Badminton is one of the few Olympic sports in which men and women can compete together.

As well as the men's and women's doubles events, there's also a mixed doubles event at the Olympics.

SPEEDOMETER

Believe it or not, badminton is the world's fastest racket sport. The shuttlecock can reach speeds of 260 km/h – the average racing speed of a Formula One car!

A WINNING TEAM

The key to success in doubles events is good communication between the two team-mates. Usually, each player has different responsibilities. In mixed doubles, for example, the female player usually stays close to the net while the male player runs around the back of the court chasing deep shots.

REIGNING OLYMPIC CHAMPIONS: Men's doubles: Ha Tae-Kwon & Kim Dong-Moon (KOR)

Badminton mixed doubles

KOREA

PLAY AREA

On a badminton court you'll see two sidelines and two baselines. In a doubles game, the outer lines are the play area, except when serving. Then, only the inner baseline counts. In a singles game, the reverse is true. The inner lines are the play area, except when serving. Then, the outer baseline counts as part of the court.

DID YOU KNOW?

The 16 feathers used on each shuttlecock must come from three different geese!

The net is set at the same height in all the badminton events — 155 cm at the post and 152.4 cm in the middle.

Malaysia won its first Olympic medal in 1992, when two brothers, Razif and Jalani Sidek, took the bronze in the men's doubles.

WHAT'S IN A NAME?

Duke of Beaufort

A game very similar to modern badminton became popular in India in the 1800s. It was called 'poona' and it was introduced into Britain by an English aristocrat, the Duke of Beaufort. The Duke played a version of poona at his home, Badminton House in Gloucestershire. The name of the house soon became the name of the game as well!

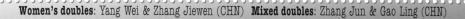

Women's doubles: Yang Wei & Zhang Jiewen (CHN) **Mixed doubles**: Zhang Jun & Gao Ling (CHN)

INDEX

Acknowledgements

We would like to thank Ian Hodge, Rosalind Beckman and Elizabeth Wiggans for their assistance.
Cartoons by John Alston.
Copyright © 2000 ticktock Entertainment Ltd.
Revised edition 2008 ticktock Media Ltd., 2 Orchard Business Centre, North Farm Road, Tunbridge Wells, TN2 3XF, UK.

Picture Credits: t = top, b = bottom, l = left, r = right, OFC = outside front cover,
QBC = outside back cover, IFC = inside front cover

AKG photo: 2/3t, 11br. Allsport: 3bl, 4bl, 4/5c, 6/7c, 7tr, 8/9c, 10/11c, 16/17c, 18/19c, 19tr, 20bl, 22/23t, 24tr, 24/25 (main pic), 26/27c, 28bl, 28/29 (main pic), 30/31c. Ann Ronan @ Image Select: 31br. AP/ PA Photos: 27b. Clive Brunskill/ Allsport/ Getty Images: 8tl. Empics: IFC. Petros Giannakouris/ AP/ PA Photos: 14b. Ramzi Haidar/ AFP/ Getty Images: 23b. Robert Laberge/ Getty Images: 12/13c. © Neil Marchand/Liewig Media Sports/Corbis: OFC. Rex Features: 14/15c, 20/21c.

Picture research by Image Select. Printed in China.